T0017079

75

FSG

PALE COLORS IN A TALL FIELD

PALE COLORS

IN A

TALL FIELD

CARL PHILLIPS

FARRAR STRAUS GIROUX / NEW YORK

Farrar, Straus and Giroux
120 Broadway, New York 10271

The Library of Congress has cataloged the hardcover edition as follows:
Names: Phillips, Carl, 1959- author.
Title: Pale colors in a tall field / Carl Phillips.
Description: First edition. | New York : Farrar, Straus and Giroux, 2020.
    Includes bibliographical references.
Identifiers: LCCN 2019046726 | ISBN 9780374229054 (hardcover)
Subjects: LCGFT: Poetry.
Classification: LCC PS3566.H476 P25 2020 | DDC 811/.54—dc23
LC record available at https://lccn.loc.gov/2019046726

Paperback ISBN: 9780374539351

Designed by Crisis

He taketh my hand / in his

CONTENTS

PALE COLORS IN A TALL FIELD

THE LAST OF FANFARE

—By fire, then, but within view of a rough sea?

Yes, he said. And: That's perfect. And: Don't stop.

Clouds moving behind leaves in front moving

ON BEING ASKED TO BE

MORE SPECIFIC WHEN

IT COMES TO LONGING

When the forest ended, so did the starflowers and wild
ginger that for so long had kept us
company, the clearing opened before us, a vast
meadow of silverrod, each stem briefly an
angled argument against despair, then only weeds by
a better name again, as incidental as
the backdrop the ocean made just
beyond the meadow . . . Like taking
a horsewhip to a swarm of bees, that they might
more easily disperse, we'd at last reached the point

in twilight where twilight seems most
a bowl designed to turn routinely but
as if by accident half roughly
over: bells somewhere, the kind
of bells that, before being housed finally
in their towers, used to
have to be baptized, each was given—

to swing by or fall hushed inside of,
accordingly—its own name; bells, and then—
from the smudged edge of all that
seemed to be left of what we'd called

belief, once, bodies, not of hunting-birds, what we'd
thought at first, but human bodies in flight,
in flight and lit from within as if
by ruin, or triumph, maybe, at having
made out of ruin a light, something
useful by which, having skimmed the water, to search
the meadow now, for ourselves inside it where, yes, though we
shook in our nakedness, we lay
naked as we'd been taught to do: when afraid,
what is faith, but to make a gift of yourself—give; and you shall receive.

PALE COLORS IN A TALL FIELD

Remind me to show you where the horses finally got freed
for good—not for the freedom of it, or anything like
beauty, though their running was for sure a loveliness, I'm
thinking more how there's a kind of violence to re-entering
unexpectedly a space we never meant to leave but got
torn away from so long ago it's more than half forgotten,
not that some things aren't maybe best forgotten, at a
certain point at least, I've reached that point in my own life
where there's so much I'd rather not remember, that
to be asked to do so can seem a cruelty, almost; bad enough,
some days, that there's memory at all, though that's not
exactly it, it's more what gets remembered, how we
don't get to choose. For example, if love used to mean
rescue, now it's more gladiatorial, though in the end
more clean: Who said that? Not the one whose face I've
described somewhere as the sun at that moment when,
as if half unwilling, still, to pull itself free from the night's
shadow-grove of losses, it first begins to appear. No.
Not that one. And not the one whose specialty was
making a bad habit sound more excusable by calling it
ritual—since when do names excuse? Wish around for it

hard enough, you can always find some deeper form
of sadness where earlier—so at least you thought—mere
sorrow lay . . . I'd been arguing the difference between
the soul being cast out and the soul departing, so I
still believed in the soul, apparently. It was that long ago.

BLUE WASH ON LINEN CANVAS,

BELIEVED UNFINISHED

And he woke again like a thief undetected, invisible therefore,
and therefore free. The bronze horse's hoof stood raised for
apparently ever about to trample beneath it the cross of wood
faced with tin half beaten half

                                    tooled to a filigree that said, or
seemed to say, that's what it takes, a violence, to get at last
even this far, mere decoration, nothing close, for example,
to those late afternoons of the sun parsing the dead bamboo like
fidelity itself

                     —no, I'd say it more was like seeing for the first time
from sea that bit of the land that you've always lived on, and watching it
slowly become more small, until maybe you lived there,
or didn't, here's the sea

                          anyway in front of you, here's the rest
(the waves whispering, as if waves could whisper), here's
what happens, not what's meant to happen; nothing's

                               meant to happen . . .

TO ALL APPEARANCES

We drove to Head of the Meadow Beach because we'd always
meant to, and never had, and we'd been wanting
to swim again.

> And we did swim,

and it was as if all those years of surrendering differently but with
equal abandon to joy or sorrow—depending on which
had come when, and in what form—had vanished:

we stood precisely at that point in being young that's
just before the moment when what we expect
is one thing, and what we hope, another.

> As I said, we did swim.

We swam until it no longer looked like swimming, but instead
more like trying to rescue whatever inside ourselves had mattered once

from ourselves, by moving farther away from it.

TUGGING THE ARROW OUT

There's a nudging that a living horse
will sometimes extend toward a dead one,
   a nudging not so much against death—what is
knowable to a horse, but not understandable—
but against that space right before loneliness
   settles in for real that horses
do, it seems, understand.
And so that was the first day.
   The night was what night always is:
a black starfish, black according to some
for holiness, to others for the limbs themselves,
   unfurling as if from long sleep or a late stiffness,
or as when a quiet thing, and very still, starts moving,
moves, one stiff black limb
   at a time.

INSTRUCTIONS PRIOR

The tickseed thriving in banks like clouds beneath us

The idea of a wind

The clean commitment every instinct comes down to in the hawk
    descending

Actual wind, waves as waves

The idea of a body

Waves as merely interruptions for once across the lake's flat surface

Only what you yourself mean to it, yes

Your idea of the world

The body as a shield keeping slightly at bay what it also reflects

Everything you've lived for

Its raised wings machete-ing the space between want and having

For hours, I lay beside him in the pear tree's shadow, watching him
sleep.

FOR NOTHING TENDER ABOUT IT

If as shame is to memory, so too desire,
then is this desire, this cloak of shadows,
that I wrap close around me, that I
refuse to take off?

But the lake looks endless.
And my boat's increasingly but a slowish swimmer,
across the waves—I've known
hurt, I mean; and I have been afraid. Sometimes

the difference between forgetting
to bring along artillery and showing up
on purpose to the war unarmed

is just that: a difference. Sometimes a lost tune,
unreckoned on, unearned, resurfaces anyway. Just because.

Am I not the animal by belief alone I myself make possible?

DIRT BEING DIRT

The orchard was on fire, but that didn't stop him from slowly walking
straight into it, shirtless, you can see where the flames have
foliaged—here, especially—his chest. Splashed by the moon,
it almost looks like the latest proof that, while decoration is hardly
ever necessary, it's rarely meaningless: the tuxedo's corsage,
fog when lit scatteredly, swift, from behind—swing of a torch, the lone
match, struck, then wind-shut . . . How far is instinct from a thing
like belief? Not far, apparently. At what point is believing so close
to knowing, that any difference between the two isn't worth the fuss,
finally? A tamer of wolves tames no foxes, he used to say, as if avoiding
the question. But never meaning to. You broke it. Now wear it broken.

SNOW

Or am I not
still the victor, who knows to look but once upon his conquests,
then away, lest he seem vulnerable, by which I mean surprised?

A LITTLE CLOSER THOUGH,

IF YOU CAN, FOR WHAT

GOT LOST HERE

Other than that, all was still—a quiet
so quiet that, as if silence were a kind of spell, and
words the way to break it, they began speaking.
    They spoke of many things:
sunset as a raft leaving the water in braids behind it;
detachment, the soul, obedience;
swans rowing at nightfall across a sky filled with snow;
what did they wish they could see, that they used to see;
to mean no harm, or to not especially, just now, be looking for it;
what would they wish not to see, could they stop seeing;
courage mattering so much less than not spooking easily—
maybe all nerve is; the search-and-rescue map wildflowers
make of a field in summer; deserving it, versus asking for it,
versus having asked, and been softly turned from.
    They said it would hurt, and it does.

SINCE WHEN SHALL

SPEAK OF IT NO MORE

—Clouds like the manes of stallions, the mane alive still
on the stallion's ghost-body. As if the body had died, I mean,
and the mane forgotten to. Or been weirdly stranded. I'm
no one's horse. I'm not what waves like a bit of ocean down
   and to either side of its brindled neck. I'm not a thing I know.

THE SAME IN SUN AS

IT FELT IN SHADOW

Crownless now, intransitive, neither at rest nor
not at rest between to be shaken and to be
less shaken, in his head he's the magnolia's
branches, he's the cast of ravens scattered loose
among them. To envy a wilderness, as opposed
to becoming one: he has learned the difference, how
all the more powerful parts to a life—as to art,
as well, when it's worth remembering—resist
translation. Whence comes their power. My
trade is mystery, this song I also call mystery,
he says to himself, half singing. As if joylessness
were technically just a word, in which
joy figures, or he ever believed as much. He has
learned the hard way. As if sensation could
stop being a ceaseless wheel once the wheel
stopped turning. He has learned the hard way,
the only way that counts here, and won't go back.

So dark the night had been, not until daybreak did they know for certain where they'd made their camp was not so far from where, days earlier, they'd broken it, the same east-facing ruins of what had been a temple once, just above cloudline. If there was shame, each put a silence to it.

One started dancing—a slowish dance, to free his legs from their stiffness, hardly helped by the cold. Another tossed what little hay was left to the horses and pack mules. Here's some water, said the third one, offering it as tenderly as he'd spoken of it, so as not to spill, For they'll need that too.

AS EASY TO CRY AS NOT TO

You in?   You out?

   To un-row the journey
has not been as simple as turning around,

rowing stiffly back, through the storms,
defeats, also victories, faces broken or
in mid-bloom spared, depending, that you thought
—sometimes wished—you'd only have to see twice:

the requisite first time, of course,
then the mix of sorrow and relief, too, which is
that second look, back from the distance of
having left what's difficult more and more behind.

To look at yourself feels no different now than looking away.

Call it loose notes on tragedy as, for once, the real thing
if you want to, but what *is* it, about spring?

WHEREFORE LESS LONELY

Pulls pistol from left holster, but right-handedly. Spins pistol.
As if one of those gestures that, though untranslatable, we repeat
anyway, despite a growing sense that with each repetition
each somehow means something less. Meanwhile, the usual moths
again appearing, mothlike, flowerlike, like those flowers from
childhood I used to call Strip Heaven, and nobody stopping—
that I remember, at least—to ask why . . . Augustine speaks
of memory as a mansion of vast halls, many-chambered, and
fair enough, that's how memory can seem, though other times more
a labyrinth of dead ends and false openings, there's a way out

—but finding it? If I tell you now there were two of them,
and that over and over, whether out of fear, against fading away,
or against having sworn to be kind, and fumbling it, one kept fucking
the other, as if all machine, if I've tried to forget, and can't,
did it happen, the leaves above them variously stilling, unstilling,
memory as a forest of leaves, then memory as the more
immediately apparent side of the leaf, rumor the paler side,

the soft lining . . . How I've loved is not how I meant to love. By
intention or fate—what I was maybe wrong to have not
believed in—it makes no difference, finally. "Whoever by now

doesn't know the wind blows more freely at the field's
farthest edge will never know" amounts to words
as camouflage—it doesn't change what's true, only what
truth looks like, which more and more comes again to memory,
whose cure for loneliness, it seems, is a kind of company that only

steepens loneliness: all the lives, all the words spoken, that can
neither be brought nor get taken back. My arrows, my lake
of swans—here; I relinquish them. I leave the stag, slow-dying,
where long ago I found it. If not out of respect, then in my name,
for pity's sake, do at least what's decent, sir, and cover its face.

SO THE EDGE OF THE WORLD

Back then, we'd fall asleep to the wind at night.
The wind was enough.
    I think we thought sleep meant rescue,
and because sleep came easily, always unannounced,
we were safe. But if safe,
    why the need for rescue?
And since when does rescue amount variously
now to the forgetting that sleep offers,
    now to dream's not-so-predictable distraction,

I almost said aloud into the room's dark all around us,
last night, though this morning these seem precisely
    what rescue comes to, or can, and my mistake has been in thinking
of rescue as something more permanent than hard distraction,
sleep's soft, impermanent forgetting.
    The wind was enough mostly—

not always. Not those nights when the wind,
as if done at last with forever having
    been a wind,
became all song instead, a song

of abandonment, a wordless one, when you abandon a thing, best

    if you can to do so utterly, without words, yet

with an outward tenderness so believable, why else

does it hurt still, even now, the mere idea

    of singing it?

BLOW IT BACK

How they woke, finally, in a bed of ferns—horsetail ferns.
How they died singing. All night, meanwhile, as if somehow
the fox's mouth that so much of this life has amounted to had
briefly unshut itself—and the moth that's trapped there,
unharmed, gone free—a snow fell: the snow-filled street
seemed a toppled column, like the one in the mind called
doubt, or that other one,

                  persuasion, the broken one, in three
clean pieces . . . Well, it's morning now. Out back, the bamboo
bows and stiffens. Thoughts in a wind. Thoughts like (but
nobody saying it): Nobody, I think, knows me better by
now than you do. Or like: The bamboo, bowing, stiffening,
seems like nothing so much as, in this light, competing forms
of betrayal that, given time, must surely cancel each other
out, close your eyes; patience; wait. Maybe less the foliage
than the promise of it. Less that shame exists, maybe, than that
the world keeps saying it does, Know it, hold on tight to it—
as if the world were rumor, how every rumor

                      rings true, lately.
When I'm ashamed, I make a point of reminding myself what
is shame but to have shown—to have let it show—that variety
of love that goes hand in hand with having wished to please

and, in pleasing, for a while belong. So shame can, like love, be
an eventual way through? There's a minor chord sparrows make
with doves that's not the usual business—it's not sad at all, any of it:
this always waiting for what I've always waited for; this not being
able to assign to what's missing some shape, a name; this body
neither antlered nor hooved—brave too, this body, unapologetic . . .

WHAT THEY DID,

WHO THEY DID IT WITH

... any room, really, across which
   the light breaks like a rough sea,
      the light washing over the walls'
colorlessness, their trophylessness,
   then the light not so much receding,
      wavelike, more like staggering
elsewhere after a fight won, but
   barely, an effect of having had to—
      before entering the room—make its

way through the sycamore leaves
   whose only constant has been
      a movement patterned, it seems,
after impatience itself as to
   which wind to bow down for,
      which to resist, or at least
try to, though leaves can know
   nothing, of course, about volition,
      in this respect the leaves are so

little different from the light,
they may as well be the light, for now
superintending the room,
its walls, its lone door half open,
to be shut carefully and walked
indifferently
away from, they
may as well be the sea
the light roughly breaks like . . .

SKYLARK

You know those days that fairly swell with triumph at having
hit your mark exactly as you'd hoped to—you can feel it—
then that slow understanding that you've yourself been hit
also, proof all over again of how akin, in its disorienting effects,
triumph is to nausea?

            Nothing's right, or can be made right, or
that's for days how it's felt, between us.

         Camouflage,
            or foliage? Intention,
                or just the way things are?
       You're far, somehow.
         And I can't see far.

MORPHINE

The long fever of summer looks like broken at last, there's
a coolness that the hours, more and more, leave behind them
as they tumbleweed their way to wherever it is
finished hours go to.
Here, finished isn't the same as lost at all,
is this true
where you are?
When I lie down in the field now—field that,
for months, by day the red-winged blackbirds
gave definition to, the one fox by dusk, missing half
its tail—I'm the dropped sword in a glittering detachment
of raised ones, which is (never mind how it feels)
maybe as it should be, though sure I've thought
to worry, having long been both things: the cigarette
casually let go of at the field's center; the field on fire.

To remember at this point the carefulness
with which the survivors had arranged the fallen along
the public square's four edges where there used to be
walls, parts medieval, the same

square across which I once ran after you, like someone
desperate, has made it seem like nothing,
but it was not nothing, the seeming
desperate, the running after you,
that I called your name.

Faintly. Calmly. Less faintly.
Sound of oars finding water, coming up for air again,
though not a skiff in sight.
They say frenzy will get you nowhere.
But they used to say that about fear, too.
Rustle of wood doves in the catalpa. The catalpa's
reflection in the river it shadows. In the shadowed
river. They say here's where he first landed—god of healing,
on horseback, on his raft of ivory, bringing sleep for cure.

BARBARIAN

—That moment, for example, when you've left someone,
even knowing you could stay with him and it could work,
and there's no one else, nothing like that, still you don't
go back, is that what's meant by free will, or is that
fate—what it's been
all along? Sometimes—even here,
in what's hardly, by now, the early part of the second half
of my statistical life, where I've figured out how to be
mostly alone, left alone, as in that's how I want it—it's
        as if I've let myself down, which only has to mean
I've expected too much of myself—"of," not "for"; about
that much, I think I'm still quite clear. Likewise,
like being told to write a love poem without images
can seem the only way I've known how to love a person,
but that makes it sound like a bad thing. That
can't be right . . . At this time of year, the best light arrives
just before nightfall. It's when the trees seem most
        what they've always been: trees not questioning
their necessarily unpersuadable selves, trees beneath
which, after storms especially, I find the occasional
downed bird, dead or, more difficult, still dying. Who can
say what it counts for, but I believe

not nothing. That I've rested my head
on the ground beside it. That in
what was left of the light I sang to it. Hush now.
You're not the first piece of gentleness to have crossed this hand.

EVEN IF SLEEP AND

DEATH ARE BROTHERS

Two children feeding what appears to be a baby goose.
Of beaten gold—gold beaten
to a thinness like that of paper—a woman's
funeral mask. A satyr, feeding
a baby satyr. A field of battle, lone harpy
in the sky above it, to say death, closing in, even as
the distance between longing
for the not-yet-experienced and for what's already lost
keeps diminishing. In one version,
Achilles has no idea that the warrior he's killed
is Penthesilea—a woman. He lifts the helmet off
by its gore-spattered plume, he falls
immediately in love with her stopped face.
We swam too soon; or we swam
too far. As if gracelessness
were as easily avoidable as knowing
when to give in, finally, and no one cared
about grace. I've made enemies, should I make
peace with them? Where am I? Let whoever
loved me, by remembering, prove it. Will my son survive?

YET NO LESS GRATEFUL

Woke feeling like a Minotaur: hot, torn,
not so much undecided as undecided *upon*, and badly:
what can I possibly do now about what I am, if I'm what I am?

Like mistaking death for what's finally just proof of death—
the latest stubbornly unvanished body beside the road that the wide,
now sightless eye unstares across—
to rewrite what's been given is not refusal is no one walking away.

Between trust and what trust equals, between that and everything
I say it does, why not do whatever?

They say the difficulty with nothing-but-light,
as with utter darkness, is not so much that we cannot see,
but that we're stripped of context: we're as near
as far; all the waves stand frozen. I can't stop thinking of the future
as the past, imitating a god.

IS IT TRUE ALL LEGENDS

ONCE WERE RUMORS

And it was as we'd been told it would be: some stumbling wingless;
others flew beheaded. But at first when we looked at them, we could
see no difference, the way it can take a while to realize about how
regretfulness is not regret. As for being frightened: though for many
animals the governing instinct, when most afraid, is to attack, what about
the tendency of songbirds, in a storm, toward silence—is that fear, too?
For mostly, yes, we were silent—tired, as well, though as much out of
boredom as for the need to stretch a bit, why not the rest on foot, we
at last decided—and dismounting, each walked with his horse close
beside him. We mapped our way north by the stars, old school, until there
were no stars, just the weather of childhood, where it's snowing forever.

SAID THE HORSE TO THE LIGHT

To enter the room is to know at once how it not so long ago
contained fear. Is to understand hesitation both ways: as a form
of worry, and as but a sign for it. Through the room's lone window,
it's that ragged end to the season
when to find a sycamore
means watching for the bark's tendency
toward scab; if birch, then the bark unfurling, less
like a ship's sails than like the worn-to-parchment-thin stages
of a landfall won barely: hard the crossing,
and only some survived . . . Sometimes, to trust
the sea isn't so much the point, anymore, as to know—
without minding it—the sea's indifference. There's a series of
rooms where everything between what I remember of us
for a time took place—each room
like this room; not much larger.
Not that I'd go back there.
Not that the names that we used weren't our own,
but that we didn't need names, when I'm moved at all.
How precise and absolute I was, and—almost as if therefore—how
unspeakable. The sea itself. Arguing neither for loneliness, nor against it.

THE STEEPER THE FALL

Like this, he said, and we watched him reach for yet another fistful
of straw and scatter it, filling those patches where the grass hadn't grown
in enough. One half of me kept wanting to imagine him covering some
shame by now unacknowledged because barely

                                      felt anymore, though
understood, instinctively, as never too far away; the other half
kept still. Think of it like camouflage, he continued, People think camo,
they think it's all about hunting. It ain't. It's about

                                      not being seen. Just
beyond him, ravens staring down the field in general for any stray
particulars seemed to wait for any of us to contradict him. No one did.
In the dream, it's another time,

                         earlier in history, you can sleep outside
in the open country and wake as you fell asleep, untouched, nothing
missing, whatever regret or happiness as unchanged as the lake's face
on a day without wind—

                     but this wasn't that dream. More like love,
falling into it, what I'd heard about the falling, how it's separate from love,
that it's love itself that prevents our remembering this until it's too late.
You got something to say about it, he asked, looking vaguely
toward all of us. Then he looked straight at me.

NOW THAT NATURE

INCLUDES OBLIVION

It's almost starting to ring true again,
about fear being the sturdiest bond possible between
      any two people: I've never been
    so frightened; I've never felt
more close. You make shelter—I mean the kind
      the mind sometimes misses especially—seem no
    harder to find than those stranded-looking nests I see
everywhere, now the orchard's leaves have
      all but finished falling . . . Have you noticed it
    too, how the present tends
at once to eclipse and
      reinforce the past? Sometimes, when
    the backdrop of winter sky behind the trees'
bare branches goes red at sunset,
      I think equally of stained glass and of one thing
    making up for another—and I can't
decide. There's a hawk whose power
      lies less, finally, in its physical strength

than in its keen ability to exploit weakness. It rarely soars.
The air around it in flight can seem most like a shirt
        unsettling loosely around a body utterly
    indifferent to shirts, shirtlessness. The pearled
chest is unmistakable,
        even from the ground.

OVERHEARD, UNDER

A DARK ENCHANTMENT

Compassion first, we were told—and if that won't work,
compassion's shadow, pity, to smooth what's rough.

We find
just holding the victim's hand, lately, has been exactly enough.

GHOST CHOIR

What injures the hive injures the bee, says Marcus Aurelius. I say
not wanting to hurt another, this late, should maybe more than
count, still, as a form of love. Be wild. Bewilder. Not that they
hadn't, of course, known unkindnesses, and been themselves
unkind. When the willow's leaves, back again, unfold all along
their branches, the branches routinely in turn brushing then lifting

away from the pond's face, it's too late. Last night I doubted as I've
not doubted myself in years: knowing a thing seemed worthless
next to knowing the difference between many things, the fox from
the hounds; persuasion from the trust required to fall asleep beside
a stranger; who I am, and how I treated you, and how you feel. So
that it almost seemed they'd either forgotten or agreed without

saying so to pretend they had. Did you know there's an actual plant
called honesty, for its seedpods, how you can see straight through?
Though they'd been told the entire grove would die eventually, they
refused to believe it. The face in sleep, like a wish wasted. To the wings
at first a slight unsteadiness; then barely any. What if forgetting's not
like that—instead, stampeding, panicked, just a ghost choir: of legends,

and rumors, of the myths forged from memory—what's true, and isn't—
that we make of ourselves and, even worse, of others. Not the all-but-
muscular ache, the inner sweep of woundedness; no. Not tonight. Say
the part again about the bluer flower, black at the edges. I've always
loved that part. Skull of an ox, from which a smattering of stars
keeps rising. How they decided never to use surrender as a word again.

IF IT MUST BE WINTER

Not crowns,
not conquest defined in terms of how many fear you, or
fear to say otherwise, not by these
will you know your own royalty, but in smaller ways, how
to the least gesture there's more power than seems reasonable,
though it will feel deserved . . . So I was told, and they have not
proved wrong. I've but to open my hand,
bees come to it, the slick fur of bees
assembling as toward an honor in no way expected

though each time the honor remains mine, as if
almost it should, as if certain privileges had to do with destiny—
Do I believe that? Do I? My hand a sea
across which the wings of the bees flash
like signal flags whose patterns, instead of translating,
I make up my own translations for. I shall do as I please.
As a lovely argument can make a difficult truth
more clear, if not more sweet, though is there not
a sweetness to clarity that can almost make the truth

seem worth it? To say I'm not quite sure makes me no less
king, here. Sometimes, I open my hand and there's no sea at all,
just a windy plain, what appear to be dust storms crossing it

turn out, on reaching me, to be the disappointments—
all of them—that I never intended, each one
on horseback, my cavalry, each face
raised toward mine, as if awaiting command—
hungering for it. Forgetful, or stupid. I can see
no difference.   Look away from me. I haven't said you can look at me.

CADENCE

To be honest, the crowd frightened me at first:
the size, but also how some had—for mouths—just holes
at the back of which, only half discernible,
so that I'd think I'd seen a thing and have to look again,
lay a faint glow, like the last
embers of a fire once believed
untamable . . .

            More often than not, mystery rules out
familiarity; that doesn't mean it has to. Just so: one of them,
slowing down, stopping, laid his hand on my chest. How fair a hand
it was, despite signs all over it
of a life spent working hard in the open air. One of his eyes
spoke despair, the other brimmed with that unmistakable color
of a jetty's rocks at waterline after
so many years of waves crashing over and against them: not green-to-black,
the rocks, not black entirely, not apology, not
quite rescue. I pulled his hand away, gently—
gently enough, I think—and let what should keep falling.

TO BE WORN OPENLY

AT THE WRIST, OR AT

THE CHEST AND HIDDEN

If I believed in a god, he would be a sea-god, like the sea
in its predictability—now approach, now recede—beneath
such a god I would not mind, I think, being the shore, say of the sea
what you will, it's the shore that endures the routine loss
without which what strategies would there be for softening
the hollowness that any victory, give it time, comes with,
how curb the risk of arrogance, with its doomed but
not undangerous hound, complacency?

                                        . . . I made this for you—
put it on. I know it's not going to matter whether the decisions
I made were the ones eventually I even meant to make, or
should have, or should have thought maybe more than
twice about. What's history anyway, except—according to
the latest mouth saying so—just what happened: I flourished
undramatically, to no apparent purpose, like pretty much
everyone. The sea dragged the shore; the shore suffered the sea.

ON MISTAKING THE
SOUND OF SPURS FOR
BELLS APPROACHING

By then, of course, they'd done plenty in the name
of recklessness—their word as well, though incorrect,
for wilderness. Ah, scutch-weed, rushlightitude, if not,
why not, strowbegone, nor sheep, fa la, shall
    graze. The way, incredibly, for most it's still enough
to have noticed a similar weather pattern between
regret and the treeless plains of remorse, like that must
make them the same, or should, or at least no more
different than a fetish for being eaten alive and
whole is, apparently, from the desire to leave loneliness
    behind forever—a reasonable desire, I suppose, but
in the end a useless one, since actual loneliness isn't
leavable: love distracts from loneliness, it doesn't
crowd it from view . . . Some could almost see this,
eventually; others chose not to. Some—the luckiest—
    arrived at, then clung to, that point in love where
to be understood entirely stops being the main thing,
or a thing at all, even. They could let the nights unfurl

before them, one after the other, each a seemingly
vast underworld of damage they didn't have to talk about,
    not anymore, they agreed
it was there now, they hovered over it, what light there was
was their own.

DEFIANCE

Some say the point of war
is to make the need for tenderness

more clear. Some say that's an effect of war, the way
beauty can be: Homer's *Iliad*, for example; or—
many centuries later—how the horse's head,

to protect it in combat, would be fitted
with a shaffron, a strip of steel,
sometimes mixed with copper, all of it

hammer-worked, parts detailed
in gold. I love you, as I've

always loved you, one man says,
meaning it, to another. That doesn't make

love true. This only needs to be troubling
if we want it to be. Our minds are
as the days are, dark

or bright, says Homer, the words like coral bells
in a pot made to look like the head of an ancient god—
a sea-god, moss for seaweed across the old

god's face. To believe in ritual in the name
of hope, there lies disaster.

And turned to him.

And took his hand—the scarred one; I could
feel the scars . . . Little crowns. Mass

coronation. For by then all the lilies on the pond had opened.

NOTES

"For Nothing Tender About It": I owe the phrase "is this desire" to P. J. Harvey's album of the same name.

"As Easy to Cry as Not To": The title is my variation of a line from Henrik Nordbrandt's "On the Plain," in *Selected Poems*, trans. Alexander Taylor (Willimantic, CT: Augustinus/Curbstone Press, 1982).

"Blow It Back": For the idea of shame as a form of wanting to belong, I'm indebted to a passage in Saleem Haddad's novel *Guapa* (New York: Other Press, 2016): "I didn't despise my shame. I had no reason to do so. My shame illuminated my intense attachment to the world, my desire to be connected with others."

"Even if Sleep and Death Are Brothers": I owe the imagery here to a visit to *A World of Emotions: Ancient Greece, 700 B.C.-200 A.D.*, an exhibit at the Onassis Cultural Center, New York, spring 2017; the last few lines are funerary inscriptions from the same exhibit. Thank you to Jonathan Galassi, who insisted I see this exhibit.

"Now That Nature Includes Oblivion": The title is a line from part 34 of Mark Strand's *Dark Harbor* (New York: Knopf, 1993). On fear as a bonding force, and on the relationship between physical force and mental acuity (in predators), see J. A. Baker, *The Peregrine* (New York: NYRB Classics, 2005).

"Ghost Choir": "What injures the hive injures the bee" is from book 6 of Marcus Aurelius's *Meditations*, trans. Gregory Hays (New York: Modern Library, 2002).

"If It Must Be Winter": The title is from a line that ends Linda Gregg's poem "Part of Me Wanting Everything to Live," in *The Sacraments of Desire* (St. Paul: Graywolf, 1991).

"Defiance": "Our minds are as the days are, dark or bright" is from book 18 of Homer's *The Odyssey*, trans. Robert Fitzgerald (New York: Farrar, Straus and Giroux, 1998).

ACKNOWLEDGMENTS

Many thanks to the editors of the following journals, where the poems herein first appeared, some in different form:

Academy of American Poets/Poem-a-Day: "Dirt Being Dirt"

Boston Review (online): "Defiance"

Boulevard: "Cadence," "Since When Shall Speak of It No More"

Callaloo: "Now That Nature Includes Oblivion" (as "Now All Mistakes Conspire")

The Hampden-Sydney Poetry Review: "Snow"

Horsethief: "Even if Sleep and Death Are Brothers"

Hunger Mountain: "Morphine"

The Kenyon Review: "Pale Colors in a Tall Field," "The Same in Sun as It Felt in Shadow," "So the Edge of the World"

The Nation: "Blue Wash on Linen Canvas, Believed Unfinished"

New England Review: "The Steeper the Fall," "Wherefore Less Lonely"

The New Republic: "If It Must Be Winter"

Plume: "The Last of Fanfare"

Poetry: "Blow It Back," "Ghost Choir," "A Little Closer Though, if You Can, for What Got Lost Here," "On Mistaking the Sound of Spurs for Bells Approaching," "To Be Worn Openly at the Wrist, or at the Chest and Hidden"

Provincetown Arts: "Overheard, Under a Dark Enchantment"

The Southeast Review: "Skylark," "Yet No Less Grateful" (as "Field's Farthest Edge")

The Southampton Review: "On Being Asked to Be More Specific When It Comes to Longing"

Tin House: "Instructions Prior," "Is It True All Legends Once Were Rumors"

Vinyl: "For Nothing Tender About It," "Said the Horse to the Light"

West Branch: "Barbarian," "To All Appearances," "What They Did, Who They Did It With"

Plume Poetry 6 (anthology): "As Easy to Cry as Not To" (as "When I Heard You Were Dead, Heraclitus")

"Tugging the Arrow Out" appeared on *Love's Executive Order*, an online site of weekly poems on the forty-fifth U.S. presidency, curated by Matthew Lippman.

"Barbarian" also appeared as the featured poem on *Poetry Daily*, December 26, 2018.

"Blow It Back," "A Little Closer Though, if You Can, for What Got Lost Here," and "On Mistaking the Sound of Spurs for Bells Approaching" received the Levinson Prize from *Poetry*.